Through the many literary readings, annual pilgrim-ages, and sundry avant-garde events, Roy flitted and darted like an exotic dragonfly.

He had an alpha-wolf appetite for all aspects of life, and this was characterized prolifically in the various art forms he expressed himself in. Words to describe him: intelligent, teacher, as interested as he was interesting, hand-some, lighthearted, joyful, introspective, whimsical, a jester, and one of the most sacred beings I have ever come across.

His poetry, like the man, was beautifully constructed, with equal measures of reflection and spontaneity. He had great composure of mind, which I think made him share fewer of his opinions and therefore lean more towards ruthless truth. He wasted no time—in particular, this is true of his poetry: all sail, no anchor. I hope that you will come to know poetry through this collection, and perhaps the exotic dragonfly will alight on your soul.

—S. Gili Post

Neptune On High

Neptune On High

Roy Lucianna

FCP

Full Court Press
Englewood Cliffs, New Jersey

First Edition

Copyright © 2014 by Estate of Roy Lucianna

Published in the United States of America
by Full Court Press, 601 Palisade Avenue
Englewood Cliffs, NJ 07632
www.fullcourtpressnj.com

ISBN 978-1-938812-20-0
Library of Congress Control No. 2014932401

*Editing and Book Design by Barry Sheinkopf
for Bookshapers (www.bookshapers.com)*

Cover Art, "Chi Painting," © 2005, by the author

Author Photograph by David Sheinkopf

Colophon by Liz Sedlack

ACKNOWLEDGMENTS

Previous appearance of the following poems is
gratefully acknowledged:

"I'm Crazy for Stupid Sex," "Song of the
Werewolf," 1996, *The Rift Arts Forum Publi-
cation, Surfacing*, August-September.
"I Smile for the People," "Her Name? I'll Call
Her Jane," 1996, *The Rift Arts Forum Publi-
cation, Reaping*, October-December.
"Orion," "Erect on the Earth," 1997, *The Rift
Arts Forum Publication, Exploring*.
"Miss Eggwhite," 1997, *Paramour*, 4 (2).
"The Big Payback," 1998, *The Rift Arts Forum
Publication, Evolving*, April.
"Poem with an Adult Theme," 1998, *Curare* 8.
"Letter to Heine," "*La Noche de la Española*," *The
Rift Arts Forum Publication, Illuming*, 2(2).
"Empty Vessel," 1998, *Curare*, 8; *Beyond the Rift:
Poets Of The Palisades* (Poet's Press, 2010).
"The Matchsticks", 1999, *Medicinal Purposes*, 44.
"Divine Fire," "Song of Casanova," 2010, *Beyond
The Rift: Poets Of The Palisades*.

Editor's Note:

Roy Lucianna had committed himself to publishing this volume and chosen about half the poems in it before he died on September 9, 2013. I am pleased beyond measure to have fulfilled that commitment for my *sifu* in his absence.

I owe a debt to all those who enabled me to do so. First, I want to thank Eugenia Koukounas, and Linda Lucianna, Roy's sister, for helping Roy with his selection while he was strong enough to do so. Second, I want to express my gratitude to Joel Allegretti, Caterina Belvedere, Richard Donatone, Denise La Neve and Paul Nash, and John J. Trause—who were far more familiar with Roy's work than I—for going with me through the remainder of the material that Eugenia organized from the body of work Roy had put aside to be reconsidered for this book, and for their editing and proofreading efforts. I also want to thank Joel for providing its outstanding thematic structure, Caterina for checking Roy's Italian, and Paul for his suave preface.

Finally, I am most appreciative that Karen Lucianna, Roy's widow, allowed the project to move forward, and read through the manuscript for duplications and typos.

For any remaining errors, I am of course solely responsibile.

—*Barry Sheinkopf*
February 2014

PREFACE

Roy Lucianna, one of our truly original voices, immersed himself fully in this world in so many ways that his influence still endures and suffuses our community, not only through his paintings, sculptures, poetry, and music, but by the legacy of his lasting friendships and his teachings of *taiji* and *qi gong*. He pursued a fully integrated life, attempting to assimilate both yin and yang, culture and nature, scholarship and sensuality, all through the lens of Taoism with its essentially archetypal, areligious, but disciplined spirituality. He also incorporated elements of Buddhism, Hinduism, Christianity, and secular humanism.

He was a founding and active member of what has come to be called the "Palisades Poetry Movement" that began in the 1990s—regularly participating in readings as a poet, as well as a conceptual and performance artist and musician, until his death. He was a classically trained artist and an art historian, well-versed in Eastern and Western traditions and noted for his very modern experimentation in several mediums. He had a knack for discovering found objects and fashioning "ready-mades," an incisive understanding of assemblage and its connection to his intended audience (e.g., Duce "for Johannes [John J. Trause] RML 2005"). He studied the interrelationships between art and poetry, particularly within the Classical Chinese traditions, illuminating the work of Wang Wei and others.

Roy liked to spend a part of each summer in Cape May, New Jersey, "going to seed," as it were, in a Thoreau-like contemplation of the natural world that involved a focused study of insects and plants and the production of new artworks. On one such trip, a praying mantis visited him and shared his tent for a week. He observed the insect's behavior and interpreted its attitudes. He described how at one point the praying mantis looked scornfully at him as it washed its face, informing Roy just who was higher on the evolutionary scale. This, and similar experiences, reinforced the idea in Roy of man's humble place in the universe—a recurring theme in Roy's poetry.

On retreats and canoeing excursions in the New Jersey Pine Barrens, Roy would often improvise around the campfire on *shakuhachi* (Japanese bamboo flute), Tibetan drum, or harmonica, and he would make sketches or Chinese brush paintings by the water's edge. In literary readings, he was known to don a Venetian mask and play soft riffs on his flute between stanzas of his poem "Song of Casanova," and to sing the Italian verses.

Music was very important to Roy. He possessed an impressive knowledge of numerous musical traditions: the blues, Child ballads, art song, country music, Indian classical music, and 20th-century avant-garde music, to name a few. He was an accomplished player of the blues harp and seemed to have a preternatural ability to coax musical sounds and rhythms from practically any object. He wrote some poems with musical compositions or genres in mind, as in "Letter to Heine," which is set to an orchestration by Robert Schumann, and in which Roy would sing two stanzas of verse by the 19th-century German poet Heinrich Heine, or "The Affair," meant to include violin accompaniment played *adagio*.

Two of Roy's biggest poetic influences were Algernon Charles Swinburne and Walt Whitman, and he would often recite or refer to their work. Humor has an indelible place in many of Roy's poems and was used to make specific points of irony, dislocation, juxtaposition, or transformation, as in "Rewrote My Past with My Present" and "Empty Vessel." His poems sometimes can appear irreverent, but there is always more to the jest beneath the surface.

—*Paul Nash*

Table of Contents

PART THREE

꩜

PART SIX

PART SEVEN

Prologue

THE WATER'S SURFACE

My words are written on water's surface.
If you are drowning,
please don't hold on to them.

Part One

Self-Made Man

I picked up once,
placed it upon a time
and lo!
I am.

Setting

I sit in my study.
A map of New Jersey on the wall behind me.
A map of Edgewater hangs in the hall.
A photo of myself
at my desk, smiling, sits on the wall behind me.

The Local Boy

I am a local boy.
Local because I was born
to the earth in a spot
not far from here—nine,
eight, maybe six miles.
Don't confuse me
with the exotic
from far-away cultures
wearing funny hats,
funny religions,
robes flowing
and devotees
following.
I am not like
the rest of us.
I am local.

Every Day

Every day,
you wake up. Every day,
you put on your clothes. Every day,
you admit
your expulsion from the Garden.
Awake! Naked! Walk forth as Adam—
you bastard—true from
the bower.

I Rewrote My Past
with My Present

Oh my god!
I wrote over my past—
by mistake—with the present! Oh shit!
I meant to save it to some disk.
It is gone.
I have nothing. . .now.

Water Goes Down

Water is low. And like Mother Teresa
water finds
a way

W

1.

I started as a seed.
You should've gotten me then.
I am entrenched.

For you, it's too late. I have absorbed
the solar source.
I have drunk
the granite earth.

Sometimes,
poetry is exaggeration. Sometimes not.

Own it:
We are here
now.

2.

You asked if I thought
God is a woman.

I looked at your breasts
and all of those curves,
those hips,

with all of those scents:
"Oh, yes, God
is a woman."

You failed to ask,
however,
if God is a moth.

My Mission

My mission,
by God:
to bring you
to God.
And if I must lick your Lassie
till you scream his name, by God,
I'll do it!
Just scream
his name!

An Angel Was Sent

An angel was sent.
An angel came to visit.

I didn't know what it was.
So I said, You look like a faggot,
and beat the shit
out of him.

An angel left
and never returned.

Invisible Man

Invisible, I suppose,
because I am past your horizon:
snout in mud rucking.

Invisible, because you can't imagine
the cruelty I deliver in the kindest package.
And the compassion that permeates all.

In deadly silence
I work, increasingly silent I play.

I cover my emptiness with a rubber mask.
The ladies kiss it—how sweet!
The eyes are cut out,
though I don't need them anymore.

I move in silence, act like a human,
wear a wrist watch, chew and swallow. . .
No wonder I tire.
Naked, I rest, full like zero.

Dawn

Once you awaken
to the light of God, you
can no longer sleep in
the night of man.

While Living

While living in darkness,
I was exposed to light,
and it was powerful and abhorrent.

Now I live
in radiance, and darkness
is my blanket divine.

Confession of a Song Bird

I'll admit it:
I've used poetry to get women.
And after I got them,
used prose to keep them.
And after they left,
used poetry to get more of them.
Thus, do I sing. . . .

Praise and Damnation

No, thank you.
I don't want
your praise
or
your damnation.

Walk On

When I am dead, and my saliva has dried
on the sidewalk, walk on.
As I do.

Mother

A good mother, when she dies, is not missed.

She prepares her children, she lives on.
They live on.

The Earth turns towards the sun and back.

To My Mother, Recently Dead

When I look out the window,
I think of you because the eyes
are the windows of the soul
and your eyes are closed forever.

When I look at the earth,
I think of you because you're buried
in it like a spent and fallen seed.

It's the third day of thunder
and heavy rain, and the water soaks,
seeps into your bed.
I lift my sights to the sky—
for relief—
you must've gone in that direction, also.
Yes, it seems you did.

I look down.
There's my foot.
It's the same one you had
—same goddamn foot!
Same flesh.

When you were alive,
everything (so much so) was informed by you
that I never noticed.

Empty Vessel

You put your faith
and stock in me,
your hopes and dreams.

I sit like an empty boat.

You fill me
with your valuables—
bags and heaps
of the precious stuff.

I sink quietly to the bottom.

Black Flag Poem

I came upon crows in winter, high up
in the bare windy trees,
like small black flags.
I walked on to the next poem.

Intermezzo

POETRY IS CONSCIOUSNESS

Poetry is consciousness.
Words are not poetry.
Consciousness is a nightlight
in the vast sea of sleep.

The duty of poets is. . .delete:
For poetry is consciousness
and words are not poetry
and the sea crosses boundaries
if it wants to—delete.

It is the duty of critics
to use words to write: For words
are not poetry, and consciousness deletes.

The nightlight shines so you know
where the wall is.
So you don't bump your head.
But the bathroom is distant,
the waters are cogent,
and you only want to sleep.

Part Two

(Distilled Essence of) Love Poem

Oh, love.
Oh, poem.
Ahh. . . .
Love poem.
Poem, poem. . . .
Love, love, love!
Ohh. . . ?
Love poem!

Good Evening, Fellow Poets

Good evening,
fellow poets.
As you know, I have often used words
to illumine the flash and glow
of the sexual act.
Tonight, I will retire
to the back room
and use the sexual act
to illumine the flash and glow
of the words.

Woman

Woman comes to me,
blown up like the moon, swollen like a bud,
fragrant as mushroom, elusive as starlight,
salt of the sea.

Man must learn to swim.

Just Because Her Ass

Just because her ass
brushed my shoulder—
as I was sitting
in a chair of reasonable height
atop legs whose height,
seemingly unknown previously
and suggestively—
touched me here and there
over the evening's
course, attenuated digits
moving softly with firm intention
lifting light-colored eyes
to catch me in a shot
from which I probably would suffer
social embarrassment
were it published in a paper
of news, my intentions nude,
as it were. . .just because
she was placed in a position
to answer my needs, in her role as waitress,
and my needs, as one
can see in the photograph, were great. . .
just because
I was thrown by her Archaic smile—
identical to the Kore
I had sworn my love to twenty-nine
and one-half years ago

in the Acropolis Museum
in the town of Athena,
and of whom I had never hoped
to hear from in the flesh
(yet, as we know, the Greeks
carved from the flesh), whose softness
now brushed my shoulder by,
one cheek, then, boldly, the other,
as she asked me if I'd like more tea,
to which I replied:
"This tea is a bit cold,
after 2,697½ years,"
and I complimented her
on her cosmic sense of humor,
which seemingly mocked
my growing-hard phallus:
But isn't this
what the gals are for, fellas?
They own that thing as much as you
(perhaps more). And the tea
she poured with added sweetness,
just because that's
what they do.
And just because of that ba-boom
of the bi-hemispheric flagellation,
it's no reason
why I should give up fifty-plus years
of accumulated knowledge, respectability,
responsibility, self-aggrandizement,
earned and unwelcome wrinkles in time,
to throw myself at her buttocks,
which, if the truth be told,

were at the height of my mouth
when I sat in a reasonably high chair,
and which grew horizontally
and seemed to greet the sunrise
as did her breasts,
rather than welcoming the sunset—
inevitable as it is—with body sinking
timely to the grave, which
I will never know
if I only would yield to the sunrise,
the same one which now, as I sit here,
forces the self-same sub-equatorial
heliotropism which I've experienced
for these few thousand years,
just because her ass. . .
just because her frame, lithe, graceful,
surrounded my stupefied face
(as you can see, I'm not willing
to give this poem up so easily)
and carried me across
the room like some helpless pup
hungry for a bone—
and now I'd like to speak of her bones:
They rotated at the cuff,
they shot smooth to the joint,
they ended in the fingers
that grazed on the field of my back
a gratification, grace. Though she is
eternal spring, I have thirty-one years
on her and hope to knock off
some blossoms for the sake
of my brother Hades, the Harvest Guy.

Just because she brushed, brushed
me, doesn't mean I will remain unaware
of the spiteful show she puts on
for her jealous boyfriend, now stewing
in a corner, with the old bastard at the table,
smiling into the ancient tea
in anticipation of some event,
which, if she can help it, will never occur.
Kore. I worship in timeless marble museums,
Kore!
Oh, Kore!

The Long Lip of Love

She goes down as easily
as Long Island iced tea.
Or maybe two or three. . .

She feels
little sorrow,
moves hips
with joy.

When she rises,
the Dark retreats
and the sun
circles the Moon.

I raise my glass to a glimpse
of her ass
and swallow the mix
to my hairy festoon.

Turn, I Ice Me

You know me:
the many-individuated snowflakes
landing on your hot skin
and losing my selfness.
I relinquish my lacy spikes
and run liquid to the lowest.
Ahhh,
hot and melting, on you,
for you,
my love.

Song of the Werewolf

spring   sprang   sprung
springen   sprang   gesprungen

Howling, I walk on the edge of our full moon,
crying for daylight,
not knowing how to love the lover,
to love without blood.
Again, I sleep peacefully at noon.

spring   sprang   sprung
springen   sprang   gesprungen

Half-crawling, I sing of my love impossible.
It becomes a song of death in the night
as I free the body from my lover's soul,
my love-pattern printed like a fossil.

sing   sang   sung
singen   sang   gelungen

Now my feet go quiet, covered over with fur.
I stalk out this lover-victim.
My guiding light is shining;
to love is to capture her.

slink   slank   slunk

schlingen   schlang   geschlafen

My soul is sleeping in the heart of the rock,
my love as wide as space,
my tail as long as the river,
my passion raining blood-filled drops.

swing   swang   swung
schwingen   schwang   geschwungen

O, solid love unmoved.
O, open air expanding,
no rhythm crosses between them
my sanguine love to prove.

ring   rang   rung
klingen   klang   gekommen

Animal-breath sounds only
fill the dead still spaces,
the love swooshing sound of Death's sickle,
deep red of the harvest wine trickle.

wring   wrang   wrung
ringen   rang   geronnen

In blackness, my blank empty purpose,
after the flow of life,
swift fishes caught in the net.
I was there and her life is ended.

spring   sprang   sprung

springen sprang gedrungen

My blood is flying through my talking, stalking.
I am purposeful on the land.
I have no brothers to keep
and must keep my love-scent walking.

shine shone shunned
schwinden schwand geschwunden

The sun is above the earth,
the moon buried deep in the ground.
The sun has entered my nighttime
to shine on my flame too soon.
It has vanished, and I am left
without knowing how to love.
Again, I sleep peacefully at noon.

Her Name? I'll Call Her Jane

How she came to penetrate me.
I, the predator, the wolf,
who knows all the doors;
the intelligence of extreme hunger,
the quest for lifeblood.
How did she come to penetrate me
with her sea-and-air eyes,
her targeted gaze,
her will?
Comest thou of late from
Albion's fair shores?
And many bitter miles since
hast thou ridden?
She lanced me.
In an instant I was off my horse
and rolling in clanking armor
to avoid the insistent hooves,
the dangerous thunder
of my own horse,
my fine filthy steed,
also uprooted by her sweet
charger mount.
We have been catching our breath
and looking for a new pennant.

On the Cultivation of Roses
in the Northern Hemisphere

Your eyes half-closed—half-closed in love.
I peer but cannot see.
I thrust but cannot enter.
Yet, no one is more inviting: the garden gate
open,
the smell of earth
and roses,
the gardener and her secrets
always in the shed.
Your eyes fully closed, fully closed in love.
You brought me satiation.
I brought footprints
to your soil.
You fill them with plaster
and hang them on the wall.

You, Burning

You burned like extremes
when you entered my atmosphere.
Don't blame me.
I revolve my molten core. I open the core
of my sun like fire
and moths
and breasts
around nipples.
Besides, I attract
a lot of space junk and can't keep track of it all.
Besides, I am singular and spinning
and producing O and O_2.
You streaked like comets
when I slowed you down.
Open to gravity
or perish.

Future Poem

Like Nelson Rockefeller,
I fucked that young thing,
rolled off the bed,
and died on the way down
to her Oriental carpet.

She talked to the press afterwards.

Song of Casanova

I am Jacques Casanova,
Chevalier de Seingalt, Knight of the Golden Spur,
and I tell of my lineage:
. . .but why bother?
My friends, of course, are much renowned:
I was received, of late, by Madame de Pompadour,
have spent days on end
with the illustrious Voltaire, and have stood tall
in the company of popes and of kings.

Besides, in necessary conditions, I can lie better
than most can tell the truth
(for I am, above all, *un litterato*). Yet truth
is the only God I have adored.
Those not truthful to themselves
are not worthy of a life:
Their love is lacking.

Fear and hatred kill the unhappy wretch
who delights in nursing them in his bosom.
It keeps him
in professions of persecution and moralization.

I am fearless, fulfilled, full with love,
and a man of letters.
Though letters may lie, the body, this body,
speaks true.

I have entered,
o, I have pushed my way
into the highest societies.
I have tried—I contrived, controlled—and I knew
they would lose their heads (as I lost mine
more than once),
so I proceed—*io vengo*, I come.
You open the door
you didn't know you had, and in I come.
I would be the unseen seed
of the Holy Ghost
to your Blessed Mary Ever Virgin,
if only. . .if only.

These are times of Enlightenment,
of immediacy and reason,
here in the boudoirs, and now,
right now!
But if you blush in your blue veil,
Venere pudica
then I approach you from behind,
the *Palio* pounding in the street,
shouting, stampeding, the dust
and the dust!
We watch on the crowded balcony
where nobody sees; I raise voluminous fabrics
and I plug you with ease—thus!
from behind, slowly and quietly
from behind.
We bump in the midst of society—
like bees in your garden,
like winter to spring.

Futile! the many wigs and powders
and laced-up bodices
and floor-length folds
they put between us,
I drum.
And you, o you contain yourself
beautifully, *cara*,
my secret shaft, your soft rump round.

But I remind you, I am a literary man.
Now a shriveled prick
of a librarian at Dux,
provincia di barbaro!
I love my books. . .fucking. . .books!
The duke doesn't mind.
I. . .make. . .my way as I can.

And I write: O Venezia!
Crystal clear city, my city,
you foggy fragrant mist.
You bulbous humped
whore of snaking glitter.
O you stink, O fragrant lover!
You imprison me,
you rape me;
I raped you.
I reaped the flower and,
yellow-thighed, sighed through the night.

This is my ground, my watery ground,
my view on the *Histoire de ma vie!*
I struggle in your tight alleys

between your tight thighs—
Non me ne importa—dammela!
Give it, just give it!
And I will return it
four-fold.

I am your erect domes—
your hidden bones
in your darkest hole—
the living *cappela delle ossa.*
I am your San Marco to the moon—
Byzantine and somewhat berserk.
Your *barca—your barca*
in the canal flowing,
I am your campanile, *lungo,*
your grand cock, till dawn crowing.
I am the hopeful inhale
to your Bridge of Sighs.
And yes! I complete you:
fire to dry your dampness
water to hiss my fire
steam-driven pistons,
machine of desire.

I know what you want,
and I am what you want.
Sono. . .desiderio.
Sono il tuo desiderio.

My wit, my sharp rapier wit
cuts clean the heads
of the *ancien regime.*

Daughters, wives, moneyed crones
fall prey to this sword,
respirating hard, then soft,
then hard, then softly sliding the nape
of her neck;
I have my eternal way, she her way
to eternity.

Do they want it? I mesmerize.
When do they want it?
I astrologize.
How do they want it?
I show them how they want it.
Così, così. . .fottan' tutti.

Your winding stream of fragrance has led me
through this life, Henriettes, all—
your scent now distilled
yet opened and bulbous like cognac in a snifter.

Self-righteously,
you ask if I regret.
I think not.

*Martir d'amor
non dura che un giorno sol';
piacer d'amor
dura tutta la vita.*

The Affair*

And when it was all over and done with,
he thanked me
for making his wife a better lover.
I graciously accepted and asked him
if he had, perhaps, a daughter?

*accompanied by some adagio violin music—
Beethoven string quartet?

Miss Eggwhite

Her name was Prissy Eggwhite,
I loved her all the more,
We rocked and rolled
till she cracked one day,
And I licked her off the floor.

•53•

A Rose

Sure enough,
a rose is a rose.
It is only half or perhaps less
without a nose.
How much
do you bring?

True Love, Short and Lasting

I loved her
fresh and sweet
as a plum.
And later,
as a prune.
True love,
short and lasting.

Circular

I swear you off. Like liquor,
like bottomless pungent wine,
I pull my cork from the mouth
of your bottle—PUBP.
I screw it back in tight,
lay the bottle down: Soak, soak it.

I swear you off.
Banging like a heavy head before noon.
Painful suns through my eyes
scorch the back of my skull.
My lids close heavy,
your pants slide rounding down the back
and there you are: double-faced,
white like the moon,
secret like the night,
sexual as an orbiting sphere.
Circular like love.

I swear you off. The birds by day,
two glasses in the sink,
the pain in the windows of my soul,
the shattering joy of wine even splashed
on the shirt.
Even buttons through the hole know
the circular joy—of fastening.
I swear,

as night loosens the muscles
of my tongue,
I swear,
as a hair pokes long through
the clenched teeth of my zipper,
the birds by day,
the wet worm sliding easily
from his hole,
the sure love of the beak,
the capturing moon,
I swear you off.

Caught in the throat,
expelled by a cough,
your tongue circling my brain,
I swear you off.

'Cause I Was Me

You liked me 'cause I was me.
"I love you. You're so free!"

So you made me your very own,
and kept me close at home.

Now I'm fat,
secure, and happy,
and I mourn my loss of liberty.
You love me differently. . . .

Short Poem

Die
a slow death with the one you love.

Refinement

She was rude, even to the point of cruelty.
She had the most excellent
manners.

These Women

These women come around,
make me a wolf.
I come walking around in my boy clothes—
and then—
I come walking around in my man-sized clothes.
I'm clear,
I'm just clear.

I'm just on the earth to eat and sleep.
I'm just here on earth to live and die.

But these women come walking around,
make me a wolf.

Intermezzo

POEM WITH AN ADULT THEME

That relationship
was about three things: me,
the head of my dick,
and my mother when I was a little boy.

Part Three

Seed

I started as a seed.
You should've gotten me then.
I am entrenched.
For you, it's too late. I have absorbed
the solar source.
I have drunk
the granite earth.
Sometimes,
poetry is exaggeration.
Sometimes not.
Own it:
We are here now.

Divine Fire

I lit a light.
So sorry you caught fire, burning and raging,
transforming and returning to charcoal
like Saint Joan
in her
transformation
to sainthood
from
medium
rare.

Name Me

What is this pain, attached to my name,
that follows me, buries me,
in senses on fire, to the night
and the morrow and the night?
Call me now
(if you know how to call me)
Man caught in woman.

Consummation, Consecration

Real love consumes like fire.
It grows with life, can flicker,
can die.
Divine love consumes, will not waver,
will not be put out, by and by
and by.
Burn now! Burn.

Wet and Dry

The space between us like solid.
We are both in the room.
The space between us solid.
You move,
it moves me. You inhale, I exhale.
You open,
I am in.
No space between us.

I and You

You live in an igloo.

You use blocks of ice to keep you warm.

I came for a visit. Well, I said,
whatever the climate allows, to keep you warm.

OK.

I left in a day.
(Earth is an interesting place.)

And I?
I left in a day.

And you?
. . .relatively warm.

The Marrow

I can't help it: When I see you
I chase my tail.

Bite.

When I catch you in my eye-ray, it moves
like free will.

I am so stupid.

Bite!

Your odor
covers the Earth and mammals' hearts
beat together
as airs
still
vibrate.
And teeth
long for teeth, the lover:
your bone.

Pose for Me, Don't Pose for Me

Pose for me, if you will.
Don't pose for me, if embarrassed.

I myself am embarrassed, in life.
Pose naked for me.

They say that naked is the face of Truth.

If you can't stand Truth, leaf out and cover.

The artist
is not inspired.

Turn back, you Muse!

Poem 786

Oh, God save me!
I told my friend,
I've had too much pain.

That's the extent, she said,
of your gain.

My Peach

I had two peaches.
One I ate, the other not.
The one became me,
the other rot.

The one is now my hair,
my skin and tissue lining.
The other is turning pulp
and cultivating growth.

The one is me, the other not.

That Lump

You know that lump between my legs?

Well,
that's my brain.

And I've been doin'
a lot of thinking lately.

Now I'm the smartest dumb fuck around.

Harvest Moon:
The Leaves Come Down

Moon,
O Moon: cogent! Shine.
Shining,
conjugal,
reflect, a-a-a-a-a-a-absent S-Sun.
Letting light-drinking, spinning,
right-thinking woman of earth,
and man the same.

Reflecting heads
and breasts and gonads of same.
Moon,
I am pining my earth-ness,
my breasts the same. I pining
the loss
of my light.
Help me.
Not hot, not cold: Help me.
I have forfeited my breasts
in the operating theater
and my gonads the same. This life
of continuous shame.
Moon, Moon,
would I were made of stone
like thee.

Great Longing

Long. Longing.
Like the idea of table trapped in wood, I long. . . .

Sweet Sweet Conquer

You,
hey you.
You slipped under my radar. Congratulations.
You took most of the territory that used to be
called
"me. "
How (?) did you do that?
Anyway,
I am taken
and all of my resources are yours.
I,
a very slippery nation.
All of YOUR resources: check!

Prayer 2273

Dear God, save me from myself
and others like me.

Intermezzo

TOWARDS THE HARVEST MOON

Tonight,
the moon is bright, the sky is endless.

For better or not, the earth is one.

And. . . circle.

Part Four

Psalm 068201

I fell like the rain, unequivocal,
and you couldn't help getting wet.

This is the purity of nature
and the simplicity of nurture.

How, But Not Why, I Was Born

Your flapping mouth,
penny-wise,
pound-foolish,
keeps me sewn
into the fabric of society.

I make me respond. I do it
for you.

Now you see me:
the golden embroidered ox. But really,
I am the mind
of the needle.

July

Rich red poppies drench my blood.
Cold wind snaps my mind, too.
Tears flood my chest.
I have arrived on Earth,
Gasping, grasping.

Take my poop, oh, Mother, I can't handle it.
Listen for the song
I am yet to sing.
File your dreams, oh, Father,
And the ones you have for me.

(They won't throw me out:
I smell so good, feel so good,
Am so cute.
Not any time soon:
They won't throw me out.)
Take my poop,
And I'll give you more.

My eyes swim like glass in his cosmic sea
My brain storms lightning—fierce electricity.
I do what I must
See it, grab it, work it.

How am I doing so far?
I plow

As they plow,
I reap as they reap,
I harvest in that time
And the fruit is not mine.

I am scythed and returned to my home,
Drenched in spirit.
O Ant, O Fish, O Dog

O ant, O fish, O dog: Find me sitting on a log,
Find me the moon
In the eye of a frog, O ant, O fish, O dog.
O spider, O ox, O bird: Hear our confession
Formed into words.
Our senses so dull
With thoughts of our god, so few know Blake's
Worthy clod.
O spider, O ox, O bird.
O space, O time, O thought: Find me sitting
On a log, counting the days
Without end
In fungus and bugs, in lichens and moss, in sun
And in snow, we must rot,
We must grow,
O space, O time, O thought.

I Smile for the People

My habits
and habits of thought
and habitual ways of acting,
non-acting and re-acting,
are molded into the subtle
bone-and-flesh landscape
of my face.
I smile pleasantly for the people.
My skeleton's head
laughs wickedly inside.
He peers out penetrating,
from the deep center of his no-eyes.
He smiles for the people.

Because Moles

Because moles live underground,
I love the light and blue sky.
Because eagles glide so high,
I love the dark and deep earth.
Because primates live in trees,
I love to swim the liquid sea.
Because fishes jump and fly,
I could burrow in sand,
warm and cool, wet and dry.

I'm Crazy for Stupid Sex

I'm crazy for stupid sex
like the moth at the candle's
flame. My sex bats that flame
and dies
crazy
stupid
around and
around and
around

The Sound of Music

I dreamed I walked downstairs,
out in the cool night air.
I left my pants and, strong and hard,
I pointed to the stars.
Oh, Venus! Oh, Mars!
I walked to the crossroads
and pissed a long line.
The night air caressed me;
the night can't be wrong.
Ah, Earth! I am.
I walk the street
to the young blooming tree.
I spray Milky Way
across secret virgin
blackness to light the clear sky.
Do I fly?
Like Cygnus,
I fly.
I am string vibration,
the gut's harmonic smile;
I measure the sidewalk to curb,
and the extra mile.
I dreamed I was one of us,
the pattern and the tile.
Different, undifferentiated,
housebroken, and wild.
I don't care what you say;

I give my life
to the sun and day.

Cannot Do Enough

I call out,
having plunged
into the bloodstream
of human kind.
I move with the pulse,
call out in disbelief,
not knowing how I became
such.
I swim the secret stream
infused in cosmic spiral,
response to heartbeat,
the heartbeat of one,
the inhale of one,
the exhale of the Big Bang.
I can only call out
because I've seen too much
and cannot do enough.

The Drop of Light (Lord, Highest, I Can Never Know)

Bear me on Earth with mangled legs,
Whole and healthy of body and mind,
Or mangled mind.

Bear me as you will.

Lord, the Highest (I can't see),
Bear me here as you will.
I am here.

Bless me with abundance,
Deprive me of food,
The body ended by hunger.

Bear me on earth,
As you will,
Lord (I cannot know).

I am here.

Born of hostile people,
In a land of mental want,
In a strange land

Where no heart is present.
Love me, Lord,

And bear me there, if you will.

Born of the loving,
Born in love,
Precious and wanted,
Kissed, caressed,
They love me as I am,

Bear me on this Earth, Lord,
As you will.

For I am here.
Bear me as kinda stupid,
As the shining bright faculty star.
Bear me, Lord, as you will.

I am here
(whose choice is it?). I am here.

If I am to be a simple one,
Then give me one thing:
One drop of light
To find my way.

If showered with all the blessings.
Then just one thing more:
The drop of light.

If body eating my body to survive
And I in anguish I am finished,
Just one thing:
A drop of your light.

If I die, take me as I am.

In any case,
I come to you,
Unknowable,
As I am.

You gave me the plan, I worked it,
And now come to you.
As I am.
I worked it
And I am as I am.

I'm Tired of Being Jesus Christ

I.

I'm tired of being Jesus Christ.
The pay-off not good. And besides,
you get crucified in the end.

2.

I'm tired of being Jesus Christ.
There will always be priests, always be a Judas,
and always, the Will
of the Father.

3.

I'm tired of being Jesus Christ.
For I will always be misunderstood.

Letter to Heine *

Dear Heinrich,
I tried not to get too entwined
in it, but spring came
so quickly this year.
I really hung on
to the thick dry skin of the tree
as the commencement of wild
bursting began—green shoots
spiraling from between my toes.
And God! You know. . .twisting
roots underground. . .at first
just white and tender,
then! relentless seeking. . .and searching.
There's no place to hide.

Im wunderschonen Monat Mai,
Als alle Knospen sprangen,
Da ist in meinem Herzen,
Die Liebe aufgegangen.

You know, Heinrich,
if my equatorial belt
represents the ground line,
then my root seeks
safely in the dark,
come moonshine,
come sunshine.

And I find my break
taps nervously on the bank.
The earth tilts
more and more
towards the sun,
I spread my wings. . .

*Im wunderschonen Monat Mai,
Als alle Vogel sangen,
Da hab' ich ir gestanden,
Mein Sehnen und Verlangen!*

**Text in italics by Heinrich Heine,
set to music by Robert Schumann*

Intermezzo

HISTORY LESSON I

*In the days
before electricity
there lived a man.*

*He sat a lot
in the dark.*

Part Five

The Year You Were Born

You have a face like a '53 Buick. And lo!
That's the self-same year you were born.

You Got a Fan

You got a fan,
and you got

shit—

hits it.

I Write My Poems Drunk

I write my poems drunk.
Then I read them when drunk.
This way, the world makes sense.
Problem is:
I read them to people who are not drunk.
Dominus vobiscum.

Dogs

Dogs love us. They love us anyway.

Check It Out

Go in and check it out, she said.
But is it fun? I said.
Yes, she said.

Is it functional? I said.
Yes, she said.

But is it fundamental? I said.
Are you fuckin' mental? she said,
Go in and check it out!

Current Politics

Stimulus package?
That's easy.
I can access it
through my front pocket.
Suddenly,
The economy is growing.

Physical Beauty

Physical beauty descends
with age, drops like a stone,
and plumbs into
the earth, to merge
with the hideous visage of the corpse.

Truth

Truth poses
in the artist's studio.

She is naked
and. . .and. . .beautiful!

Shit!
She bites!

Truth poses naked
in the artist's studio. How now,
brown cow?

Ash to Ash

You suck me like some cigarette.
Gratefully, I am turning to ash.

As Unequivocal

As unequivocal
as driving rain,
by loss of faith
you hoped to gain.
And indeed
you have.

Me and Me

On seeing her,
on meeting her,
I forgot who I was.
So I became
myself.

Simple

I'm much more complex
than you,
it's true.
And also
much simpler.

Music

Music is time and freedom from time.

Music is the fruit of Time
and freedom from Time.

Happiness

Happiness is the cessation of pain,
while the thought of it remains.
Sorrow is forgetting
it will come back
again.

Big Scare (Oh, God!)
Big Scare

It was 1999.
All those nines lined up
against you: the one.

We are sorry:
Facing the millennium
is a personal choice.
And we all die together,
separately.

ROY LUCIANNA

Days and Nights
of the Living Dead

The half-dead
are born to despise the fully alive.

The half-dead comprise the drone and hum
of humanity.

The fully alive, like queens, like queens
in the hive.

•*128*•

Balls, Mama

Oooo, malted milk balls!
Many malted milk balls.
Euuuw, many melted malted milk balls.
Messy. Many messy melted malted milk balls,
Mama.

The Aural Canal

The aural canal,
The complex system whereby we hear and are
moved
and are inspired:
I give up for now. Goodnight.

Intermezzo

WHERE?

Where
does the light shine?
Where?
Where
does the light not shine?

Part Six

Erect on the Earth

Odd vertical creatures we are,
walking upright and brushing against
the earth with our two feet,
like an abbreviated centipede.
Big to us is small to brontosaurus.
Small to us is big to the snail.
What is big to us
is the micro-thin shell of habitual space,
just a shade below the Earth's surface
and just a shade above.
What is big to us is the "march of history,"
as they say
(and when they say it, Roman troops
do march all over the earth,
not so big to them
in a thousand-year reign).
And big also,
the four million years
of *Homo erectus*. . .Good Lord!
Hosanna in the Highest
has been that hard for that long
on an average night!
I've heard it said that our own sun
will destroy us in twenty-five
million years.
What will happen to my fragile poems
and other valuables?

What if I made a sculpture
twenty-five million times more durable
than the Venus of Willendorf,
using some high-tech materials?
Styrofoam.
Yes! That'll do it,
lovingly patinaed
with DDT and plutonium.
Yes! They say that'll do it.
My gift to the future.
(I think objects last longer
than deeds anyway—
unless those deeds
have been recorded on objects.)
But what future,
as our bloating, then hardening sun,
more and more constipated,
pushes out a few last rays
of happiness onto the child's
drawing of house/mom/dad/child/tree?
World without end,
Amen.

The Big Payback

And when I woke up,
it seemed just another Wednesday,
except the Indians
had come in the night
to reclaim their land
in what is now
the Ninth Congressional District,
Bergen County, New Jersey—my home.
I opened the kitchen cabinet:
Swarming buzzing bees
had come to reclaim their honey.
Thought I saw a pig
near the fridge,
bringing back bacon.
And at my kitchen window
the huge head of a cow,
black and white.
The milk, I thought.
And when all my accounts had been settled,
the inevitable question filtered through:
Whose body is this?
'Cause I've heard
that it's just borrowed
for our brief stay
here on earth.
So whose hairstyle,
whose just-cleaned fingernails,

whose hernia scar,
whose feet, certainly used,
somewhat calloused,
with a purple nail
on the big toe
where a log fell on me,
on my toe.
Whose partially developed deltoids,
whose dental problems,
. . .return to where?
And I pray the mystics
are wrong: Man is not but a flowering,
a very brief flowering
of the Earth,
from dust to the dust. . .
O-o-o-o too black for me.
It's still a sunny Wednesday.
However, I own nothing.
It's all been returned
either to Caesar or God.

Poem 9699

The air is thick with insects.
The swamp is heavy with bacteria.
The sky is nothing without you.
The clouds mimic, mimic
and mock us animals.

My vision, my objects, my perception, my life.

The blue of the sky is not even present,
yet mocks the outline
of my presence in the landscape.

Oh, blue is nothing
but a magic color in the spectrum.

I'm getting better and better
at questioning personal histories.
I'm getting worse and worse
at understanding my place
in the universe.

Living in This World

Only two things can be done
with this world: You can stay in it,
or you can leave.
And if you do stay,
would you please behave yourself?

Premonition

I had a premonition of your death
by car accident.

Suddenly, I see you coming down the long drive
to the main road. I shout, I scream,
I'm running, shouting! Stop!

Your brake lights go on,
you look in the rear view mirror
as you slip into the road.
A large truck is coming.
My God!
Your death was instant.

Gratuities of the Graveyard

I saw her first
at the cemetery.
Her body glowed
as the body
was lowered.
Late afternoon
fog and rain
were on us.
Her hair glistened
and, in the light rain,
picked up the late
and early dew
and ran blonde
and like living honey
in light
over her shoulders
and back.
The rain
ran down
so sensual
as God's own
seed in the earth.
Sure. . .it was
a tacky dress,
but her body
was God's own
creation.

And he lowered
his own
into the earth.

I'll never forget
where I first
saw her.
Thank you
for the loan.

What is television,
except a medium you cannot touch,
my outline against the sky,
the conversation
on the telephone?

The Houseguest

He was a friendly guy,
warm personality—a singer,
kind eyes, an individual.
And trustworthy.
But I noticed,
when he stepped out of the shower,
that his foot
was cloven.

La Noche de la Española

They came out of the deep cold water.
They lay on our grill.
We sear them hot and fast
till their juices spit back
at the fire below.
Lucas and I stand shoulder to shoulder,
leaning back and looking at the stars:
How vast!
Tiny echoing sands under our feet
describe our terra firma.
We sing all night.
Sing out right
to that black ocean,
foamy white lines breaking
towards us out of nothing:
one, and then one, and then one. . .
Campers' tents, planted under trees
and groves, glow from within—
red in the dark, yellow, blue.
A woman targets us in the night,
slowly walks towards us,
one hundred feet. . .fifty-five feet. . .
she wears a dark shawl over her head:
how beautiful! *Misterioso. . .escuro.*
La Espanhola, Lucas notes in Portuguese.
She quickly pulls a white cigarette
to her mouth

and fixing me with a glance,
half-whispers,
Fuego.
Frantic for some kind of fire,
we produce a match.
She cups the light and puffs, puffs,
till the tobacco glows firmly.
The stars disappear as we focus
her bright face.
We are tense.

Gracias, her Castilian,
like a slashing feather, burns.
It's dark again as she returns
to her *marito.*
We fix her in each open second
. . .forty-five feet. . .
she looks back,
the two of us, bodies fully aflame
in the blackness.
Burning, crackling—still standing.
In a voice like dried straw,
she whispers, *Fuego.*

Big Babies on the Earth

Babies on the earth.
We are the too-quickly evolved
naked infant among the animals.

Our heads too big for the pelvis,
for proper gestation.

Thus we must suckle and hug each other
naked and fleshy—
always hugging and sucking—
always crying and laughing
as the others look on—
wonder, and look on.

Poem W

The clock ticks.
Men rub their dicks.
If you want to know the facts,
these are the facts of life.
The earth turns, cigarettes burn,
and windows need washing
most of the time.
People are banging piano keys
all the world over.
In fact, at this moment,
pianos are
piano keys are. . .
the teeth.
My art is the bite.
Oh, why don't you look
into that velvet sky?
The clock ticks very slowly
there.
Decay is the saddest,
like mine with the light blue
satin, puffed, tufted—
my best suit, lying there
with more makeup than that sad
old dame in the *supermercado*—
perfumed like artificial flowers
in a vase (dusty vase),
she must smell like death.

I hold my dick and squeeze
once, gently, for every countdown.
My testicles rise slowly
to the sky like eggs, and your eggs
rise slowly likewise.
We circle the globe like a chain
of events,
like daisies everlasting,
like the sun's sentence
of twenty-five million years.
Without no brain, how can you hear?
Without no hands, how can you steer?
Float, my beloved,
and scatter. . .
earthly life is a wind
of tears.

I Hate the Seagulls

I hate the seagulls.
They won't let me eat,
eat in peace.
I am one of them,
and I hate the seagulls.
And I don't particularly like
the females,
except once a year
for about three days.
But in that nine seconds
of copulation, I love them
enough for the whole year.
A greater love than this
no man hath.

Piss I

Piss I,
long and hard,
the bowl of the toilet—
clean, friendly bowl.
I piss along,
happy, as I see my smiling
reflection in each
of the numerous bubbles,
quite large, very small,
with the head of me
and my torso in the golden
light of the urine-filled
environment.
A me in my waste,
as beer in the bubbles,
saying goodbye and hello
to my nice-hair day
and a satisfactory
expurgation at the close
of an evening of refreshment
and polite and penetrating
conversation.

The Lace Tablecloth

I sat at the table.
It was not dinnertime.
Where the plate of food
would sit, there sat
a book.
I read and removed
the book.
There sat the tablecloth.
Lace.
I read the symmetrical
patterns, centralized,
radiating, flowering,
multiplying, and soon
my brain took the pattern.
Wholeness and completion
are, I report,
satisfying
and close at hand.

A

At 1:30 a.m.,
it's a strangely
quiet night.
No one walks,
few cars pass,
one medium-sized skunk
went by me,
the raccoons have not shown up,
the moon is heavy on the earth,
and Mars is something
which we don't understand.
Why make these pictures?
In my living room,
the fish are contained
in a small tank.
I am free in the air and I travel everywhere.
In mid-Atlantic,
I am contained
in my tank,
the fish are free
and they roam ever—here,
the moon now sits
in a heavy, billowing
cloud mass and is disappearing,
the eye closing and slowly opening.
Is this important?
All light, the light on me, is hazy.

Mars shines bright.
Mars seems to be, by hand measurement,
about four feet from the moon.
Many colors surround the moon
in its cloudy nimbus—compelling.
Any light is compelling
to the human moth.
A dog barks at night.
Some animals are running
in the underbrush.

Why do I feel such
strong compulsion
to lift my head and stare,
expectantly, at the moon?
I expect. . .what?
My cat sits
on a chair
in the backyard,
calmly, looking over at the dog.
Interesting.
He looks back at the dark vegetation,
which engulfs him.
The moon is hidden
in muffled words.
But the words
newly engaged lovers
spoke then, "I love you"—
what did you say?
and it shines bright—
"I love you!"
This is a soft powerful moon.

Mars in Pisces, and the Moon also.

A dog barks at night.

Katydids are in the house
and without.
They scrape like tomorrow
never comes: Teach me.

The moon is a sleepy-eye,
but so bright and compelling,
why aren't there two of them?
So much like an egg,
with the sperm-like approach
of Mars, swimming through the uterine
haziness and substance.

Compulsion to draw such pictures
comes, not from the alcohol I've
imbibed, but from the big mother
(fucker) herself,
La Luna.

Almost full at this point,
I stay up late
watching over the neighborhood,
every window dark
and deep in sleep,
my eyes lifted, full of expectation,
hope to that hazy moon
with Mars attached.
No one walks,

no one speaks,
stirs;
they may dance in their dreams;
the moon is floated, obscured,
curled, caressed, and revealed.
It is bright
and compelling.

Tiny ants move underfoot.
Skunks hunt,
raccoons already sleeping,
and cats still awake.
A moth passes by.
Refrigerators turn off
and on automatically.
Smart lights respond
to the silent stirring of skunks
and possums.
Street lights stay on,
moonlight stays on,
dreams are churning,
activity fills the neighborhood.
All lights are out,
all cars are still;
even the wind is still.
Flowers have closed
and the moon takes over.

I Want to Go Back

I want to go back,
if only it were true,
I want to go back to the days
of Attica, if only it were true.
Yes! The Earth is round, a sphere,
and it is round like a ball of clay.
I want to go back.
They call it ancient,
but really it is the most modern,
the future, for the earth is round
and spinning like the moon and my eyeball.
The earth is like my eye, sure and true,
and rotating. I was a man and a woman
of the tree and the olive and the gods
and the truth. Go back now, O gods?
The corrective wine, the corrective reasoning,
the delicious goddesses, the masters of man,
the gods and the goddesses spinning!
But I want to be alive, and I am,
modern, and somewhat tortured.
Here we are but will, by no means,
remain.

Intermezzo

Intermezzo

Of Humans and Animals

We raise up our eyes
and pray God.
Animals stick snouts
in mud
and pray God.

Part Seven

All of Our Words Are Nothing

All of our words
are nothing compared to the empty breath.
In one inhale,
all rivers come home, all sins are forgiven.
In one exhale,
the ocean is full, love is manifest and words scatter
like the seeds
of a maple.

Precious, Golden

The seeker,
armed with savvy and Sanskrit,
full with knowledge and meditation, outlines
himself
as seeker.
Alas,
the Tao slips through
your fingers
as you
relieve
yourself.

Target

You keep singing of the target.
You go to target-singing school.
You think on the target,
you worship that target.
You sing, you practice. . .
congratulations. . .you sing.

You never hit the target,
and your teachers have never,
and never will
(though they met someone once
who knows someone who did,
it is said).

You keep singing of the target.
Amen.

The Carpet

In your rocking chair, you rock.
The world spins.
Kids twirl on a carpet, the Oriental carpet.
You look deep into it.
That night, you have a dream. You
look deep into it, falling towards
the center. Kids twirl
uncontrollably. You rock.
The world spins.

Like a Fly Caught

Like a fly caught
between the two panes,
I open the window
to shoo you out.
There! Reality
or freedom,
directly
in front of you.
Yet you remain
like a fly
caught
between panes,
buzz-buzzing
about something.

The Deep

The Deep invites you to lunch.
The Deep.
The conversation is not translatable,
is not really conversation.
Your shoulders ache
as if muscles produce rain.
Your face falls into your lunch.
Semen swims your head around,
generation is launched.

Your brain muscles stretch,
dropping your jaw.
Your tongue thrashes lazy
like whispered throaty horns.
The Deep invites you to dinner.

You are in trouble—I hear your cry.
The Deep.
Ah, God! If ever there was one!
Let it be me. . . .

I was once a swallow, you,
a raptor of swans—but you loved me anyway
(any way you could).

A Great Heaving, a Great Desire

You walk along the dark beach
into the black.
The waves, the ocean, it wants you.
It doesn't really want you.
The waves, the ocean,
it wants you.
Life is a test between your teeth
and the things you bite into.
The waves, the ocean,
it wants you.

Beggar

Your search for love, true love,
relational love, gainful soulmate
love. . . .

Like that beggar,
walking down Seventh Avenue, his hand out:
no longer any idea of how to earn money,
keep money, offer services in return.

No longer a clue,
he just. . .sticks
out his hand
and hopes
for the best.

Fear of the Cold,
Fear of the Heat

What is it?
Your fear is it.
The cogent cry
of the animal.
Her alluring scent
alarming your brain.
You run from her.
She has already
caught you.
Like a wolf,
she is in
your clothing.
And. . .grip.

Innocent Babes

Some pain
does not wash away.
That's the one
that rhymes with stain.
Innocent babes
wrapped full fresh of flesh,
belie the stain,
yet grow the seeds
of future earth pain.

Ego

You sail up above us,
like the Thanksgiving Day balloons, parading.
The wind blows your bulbous ego to and fro.
Last night you were wrinkled and deflated,
much smaller than you really are.

You are leaking
yet blowing harder.
Hot air rises.
You blow hard.
You are always deflating.

The balloon looks just like you,
yet distorted, full of tiny holes.
More air, more air, bursting at the seams and
(Bronx cheer).

Intermezzo

MAKE SYMMETRY

Make symmetry, if you will.
Praise it, find it,
but don't neglect divine
asymmetry like the weighted wheel
of the locomotive.

Part Eight

You Want a God

You want a God who is good, kind—a heart as big
as the universe,

because you are small, bitter, and nasty.

But to rephrase
(when dealing with absolutes):

Your God is good, kind,
with a heart
as big as the universe,

because we are small, nasty, and bitter.

But to rephrase:

God is good, with a heart

as big as the universe, God is kind,
he is all love,

because nasty, because bitter, because smallness.

A Common Contraction
of Do Not: Don't

Don't
confuse me
with the rest
of humanity,

nor
with your God.

Rains Reign

God rains
in the rain forest and rains not
in the parched lands
people call home.
God is everywhere at once.

The Way of Religion

Religion
gets in the way of God. God
never
gets in the way of religion.

God

God,
you of no ears, all-hearing, know:
that I have searched all ways
and no ways
for your love
in your ever-present, seemingly absent world.

God,
of no eyes, all-seeing, know:
that I have listened for your breath
in breathless meditation and breath-taking
storms.
You,
of no thought, all-sentient, pan-cognizant,
know: that I have thought you openly,
to receive you randomly.

On Earth, you hide
in equations
which don't really work.

In Heaven,
the equations hide the you
in your work.

Why do we continually ask for your mercy?
We are so small.

Earth

Earth:
the place of sorrow, plane of teeth gnashed,
truth
unbitten.

The place of the tongue wild lashing,
and truth unspoken.

The watery world,
a flower of sun's hot juice: wet tears, burnt anger.

Let us now praise beauty: spherical, green-blue
mother-like, cloudy,
cruel.

You Watch TV

Above you,
always,
at all times,
is sky.
You missed it.
Above you by day,
a veiled blue comforting cosmos,
simple in form.
By night, the fright
of time, space, and eternity.
No wonder you watch TV.

Little People Find Big Faults,
Big People Find Little Fault

Looking young.
It's the goal of the feeling old.
Doing good
is the make-up of the thinking evil.
Being interesting:
the television show
of the boring and useless.
Good manners
covers hatred.
Showing respect:
the defense of the disrespectful.
Seeking power:
the wolf of the sheep's clothing.

I am sorry we have come to this
or have we always been there?

Can No Longer Praise God

Why is God so lonely, being God,
being alone?
So many are his.

They call him the wrong name, describe
his behavior as their own.
Fail to give him glory,
for they are incapable of such song.
Of such glory.

Why is God so lonely?

God made God.
God made angels.
Man-made is man-made
and can no longer praise God.
Amen.

Intermezzo

SIFU

The Master went to heaven
unannounced and spoke to me:
If you want to be happy,
he said, be happy, he said—
and lit my revelry.

Part Nine

Knowledge II

As you expand knowledge,
be sure to contract.
Wisdom sits like
a diamond.

Like truckloads
of grapes, knowledge must be
distilled and aged
to wisdom.

Fish In Water

You seek the spiritual.
Don't ask me. Everything I do is spiritual.
You seek the spiritual.

September 4, 2011

OK. You are here. Wake up!

We all find ourselves here on Earth.
And we all wonder at times,
Why? How?

No answer. Make one up
If need be.

But rather,
I suggest you swallow the pill.

Everything on this planet
Is born of earth.
We are all related.

Stones, trees, grass, worms,
Strange bugs—all.
All related.
All children of the mother—Earth.

Swallow the pill; accept our family.

Spacey

They don't know—it's hard
being a purple and gray
space case, showing up
at the wrong time,
failing to spring ahead
and fall back,
forgetting which people
to hate and why.
They think you just fall
into it—anyone could slip
there—but no:
It must be cultivated,
like broccoli on Mars.

Genealogical Mythology

She was a beautiful woman,
with the nose of a pig.

She reached deep underground
and pulled out potential millions.
They stirred and squirmed,
but she coaxed them to the top.

And they formed the Milky Way,
and they floated like oil
in her water,
and their glistening history lived on
in that beautiful woman, nose like a pig.
Amen.

Starfish Orifice

I read a poem.
You sat like a starfish
in your belly—full.

I asked you where the sun shines.
I saw your five arms' ends twitch, slightly.

You rotate. Stars shine. You lactate,
and the beetle's juice.

It's not my poem. It never was.
I just breathe the cosmic dust—inspire. . .
I just exhale expire.

You contract, like a starfish in your belly,
and release. . .to the swelling of the ocean.

I watch and prepare material for my next poem.

Orion

The Giant Orion the Hunter
appears when the air turns cold,
pushes angular above the horizon,
intact and active,
towards the end of the year.
You might say he's some chance-cast die,
like a five,
thrown by the hand of Invisible Chaos.
Or you might say
he's some chance gathering
of deep and closer stars
in a pattern which does not exist
from any other view in the universe.
(From here, it only seems to be Orion.)
Does it matter that he inspired awe
or ridicule—the huge horny hunter,
transformed by the awesome Artemis,
pursued by the Scorpion,
pursuing the Pleiades.
Does it matter that we ourselves,
who claim this group as god or accident,
came to exist,
you might say,
by some chance?

Elemental

You are like the soles
of Moses' feet,
like the wind
from a spin,
a flower
in ice-bound deserts.

I rest in your
pitch-black, frozen,
fossilized, in sleep,
like dinosaurs do.

Your Name Is Adolph

I think
that
your middle name
is
Adolph.
Though an American,
and patriotic,
though a "good Christian,"
a Jew,
you speak
to Allah,
(sincerely)
and he is answering,
but he too
calls you Adolph.
I say this because,
when the name is called,
you answer.
You don't have to answer.

You Brushed That Fly Away

You brushed that fly away

                Drum

But I am the excrement
deposited
on your forehead.

                Drum

Big and thoughtless
as you are,
I'm sticking with you.

                Drum

Intermezzo

THE LONG WAIT

We, black and white. We, yes and no.
We, holding tight.

All manner of gray God, everywhere at once
and nowhere ever.

God
(if you like), holding tight.

Part Ten

Nothing Like Nothing

Writers: Stop your writing.
Painters: Paint it out.
Flute players: No more tooting, looters, stop
looting.
Waiters: No more waiting,
take the orders, give them waters, and wash hands
after toilet. . . please.

How I long for rest.

For empty hands
and feather-light pockets.
How I long to test
the untrod waters
of primal sources
and mindless, mindlessness.

Behold the zero: nothing like nothing.
Shape like an egg,
as still as seed,
the number of fullness minus equal parts
of greed.

How I long for rest.

Formless in Heaven

1.

I am formless in Heaven. Always was,
Always will be.

I forget from time to time,
So I can play the game of form—
Separate from God,
Even separate from my fellows.

Why? Dunno.
So I can get a break from eating bonbons
On the cushy couch of Heaven.

2.

I sit formless in Heaven.
I watch the play of my lives here on Earth.
It seems I go there to suffer
The separation from the One.
Why?

One does not find out
Until the suffering is over.

Imagine the infinite

Squeezed into the finite. Why?
Now things can move,
Subject to yin and yang
Or yes and no
Or in and out
Or good and bad.

The cost of seeing true blue
Is lack of red.
But there is also true red,
At the cost of blue.
OK.
Linear time and perception
Are the game.
Fullness is reward in itself.

Hard to move things
When everything is present
All the time.

Knowledge III

Our best minds describe
the *nunucornus*.

I am *nunucornus*.

They feel my left leg
up and down.
It stands on one long
leg.
It is written.

They run hands and instruments
Along my back.
It has no front.
It is written.

They feel my lower *cornus*.
It has a trunk like an elephant
But smaller.
It is written.

I scratch my *cornus*.
Is there anyone out there
With more feeling?

I am *nunucornus*.

Note: "Nunucornus" *is a word apparently coined by Lucianna. The editors are uncertain of the meaning, but speculate that it may be a portmanteau of nunu, Bengali slang for "penis," and cornu, the Latin word for "horn." The model for the word is a Latinate version of "unicorn," since the poem as a whole plays off descriptions of the unicorn by the classical and medieval natural historians and geographers.*

The Heart and the Mind

I would forgive you.
I am willing to forgive you.

But, really, I would spend much of my time
over how many months and years,
shoveling, shoveling out forgiveness.

Your need is great. My time is short.

The system is full with pressure, yet
it must be released slowly.

But fast-burning is the fuse
of my life.
And yours

is much, much shorter.

Lower Mathematics

5 and 1 took a walk.
5 shines like a star of heaven as 1 searches for 2,
breathing as 1,
and yearning for 3. As 1 stands alone
and stops, feeling thin, threatening to fall side-
ways, lonely for 2, curvaceous 2.

5 and 1 took a walk.
And 1 stumbled and broke in 2, heart broken in 2,
who thought of 1 and this thought became 3.

3 struggled as 5 looked on and 5 shined as
3 onerized and 1 ejaculate spilled
on the floor.

1 ejaculate snaked and 1 egg stomaed

and 2 balls and 1 cock met 1 egg and 4 was born
and died with one purpose:
to make 5.

And 5 doubled and splot
and the earth swallowed
10-fold and little 5s
were born at once,
through the mouth of 1.

Control Freak

Eva rolled over in bed
and lightly touched his arm:
Adolph, you know,
you're such a control freak.

I am not. Now roll over and go to sleep.
But, Adolph. . .I think you are.

June 2009

OK, I've heard this bullshit before:
Let's say that you don't believe in Elvis.
I can accept that
(you know that he is still alive—
don't know how, but we all know he is).
OK,
let's say that you don't believe in Elvis,
OK,
you don't believe that he's still alive.
That's your choice!
OK,
you CHOOSE TO BELIEVE
that Elvis is dead.
I must accept your beliefs.
Let's say that Elvis is dead (God forbid),
and that you are right.
Does that make you right?
Why can't you open up and listen?

ROY LUCIANNA

Squirrel

Driving slowly, I saw a squirrel, dead,
At the foot of a tree.

Squirrels love trees:
Eat their flowers,
Caress the bark,
Bed in them,
Hide in them,
Fly up and down the trunk,
Courting, playing,
Springing their branches,
Large and small,
Live in them,
Love them.

The squirrel's body,
All fours upwards
At the foot of his tree,
Was Like me,
Preparing for death. Dead.

At the foot of the things
That I love.

But really Love no longer
As I am out of this world
And onto the next.

What killed him?
No hungry hillbilly,
No viscous wolverine,
No signs of injury.

Mammalian masters of Ariel flight,
Squirrels traverse wires,
At lengths and heights
We can't feel
Yet they haven't learned
To look left and right.
Their projected path in front of their eyes—
Why look left,
Why look right?
It works for the wire,
It works for the branch,
But not for the road.

My cat is a kitten.
He crosses that road.
He also does not look.
But his ears turn left
And his ears turn right.
He is a predator.
Is that why he's right?

Sound.
Is that his key to survive?

Gibbous Moon

I really don't know
anything about it.
But the moon entered
me
through the eye
and somehow
lit my brain
belly.

I can only tell
of its size,
ripeness,
and readiness
to fall.

Amber

Like a lacewing in amber,
my soul trapped in this body.

This body, not fossilized,
Gratefully moves on.

Like a lacewing in amber,
My soul trapped in infinity.

Advice for Those Born to Earth and Still Here

Love your body
and thus others' bodies.
Love your mind
and the minds of others.
Love the sun
and its coming
and going.
Love the earth,
personal
as it is.
Try to enjoy your stay,
and don't fuck it up
for others.

Epilogue

GOTT SEI DANK

Late at night, it's God's
delight to soak me
in Scotch
and turn on
the light.
Amen.

Index of Titles

www.ingramcontent.com/pod-product-compliance
Lightning Source LLC
Chambersburg PA
CBHW022008100426
42736CB00041B/1028